Blue Cliff Record

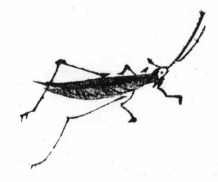

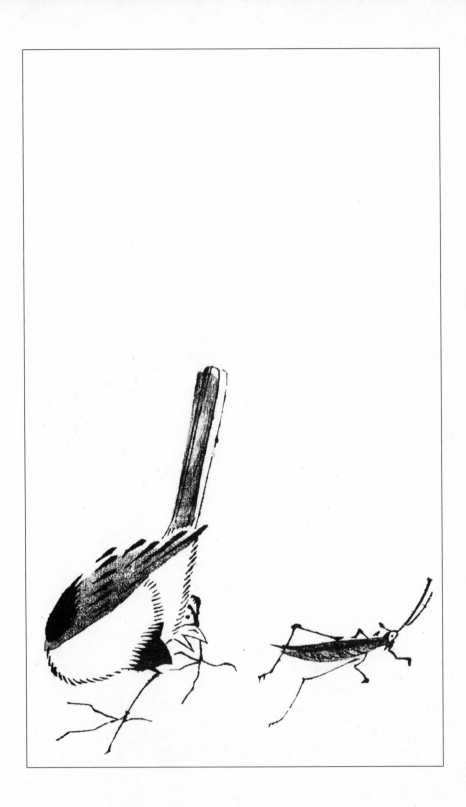

BLUE CLIFF RECORD

Zen Echoes

David Rothenberg

Foreword by Sam Hamill

CODHILL PRESS NEW PALTZ NEW YORK

Published in 2001 by
Codhill Press
1 Arden Lane
New Paltz, NY 12561
www.codhill.com

LIBRARY OF CONGRESS CATALOGING-IN-PUBLICATION DATA
Rothenberg, David, 1962-
Blue Cliff Record: zen echoes / by David Rothenberg
p.cm.
ISBN 1-930337-03-5 (alk.paper)
I. Yuanwu, 1063-1135. Pi len yu. English II Title
BQ9289.Y8213 A3 2001
249.3'927--dc21

Portions of this work have appeared, in slightly different form, in
Poetry New York, The Trumpeter, and The Kyoto Journal

This book is printed on acid-free paper.
Printed in the United States of America.

for Jaanika

FOREWORD

My first Zen teacher told me,
"Buddhism is the Four Noble Truths and the Eightfold Path. All the
rest is commentary." Nevertheless, Buddhist anecdotal commentary,
including poetry, storytelling and recorded conversations, has grown
exponentially, century by century. Other major philosophical and reli-
gious traditions have certain parallels, the vast mythology of Judaism
and Christianity sharing, for instance, the same root tales of origin.
Cultures are enriched by cross-pollination and self-examination, and
where ancient traditions intermingle and or conflict, we find our great-
est need for understanding and, often, the greatest periods of cultural
growth. A refusal to rise above dogma, religious or political, is antithet-
ical to the search for compassionate living.

Ch'an (or Japanese Zen) means
"sitting." The ancient Chinese masters brought a deep under-
standing of Taoist and Confucian classics to their Buddhist
practice and began to gather, much in the manner of the classic
Chuang Tzu, certain kinds of "tales of enlightenment" that might
serve to provoke insight in those who struggle to understand the
way and the practice of Ch'an. These *kung-an* (or *koan* in
Japanese) represent "case studies" designed to encourage mindful-
ness by breaking down supposition or defensive logic or any
number of other "barriers" to the awakened life.

All the reading about Zen in the
world gets one only about one inch down the mile-long journey of
elementary understanding. "Sitting" means sitting. But in learning to
sit daily, not in "meditation," but in "non-meditation," the mind
often can be opened through the study of (or meditation on) koans.
Some schools of Zen endorse koan study more enthusiastically than
others, but all Zen traditions acknowledge their usefulness.

David Rothenberg's "poetic echo" of the classic *Blue Cliff Record* should not be confused with literal translation. This poetic reading is equal parts reinvention and paraphrase, and embodies, as any decent poetry should and does, reflections of the sensibilities, rhythmic patterns, melopoeia and logopoeia of its author, and follows its own traditions—such retellings having existed at least since the Torah, since Homer began collecting tales in Greece and the followers of Chuang Tzu wrote down his wisdom tales. In some ways, we may see the tales of I. B. Singer or John Steinbeck and any number of others, poets and fiction writers alike, as modern parables reinterpreting biblical masterpieces. Kenneth Rexroth translated ancient Greek drama into "American Noh plays." Thomas Merton translated Chuang Tzu into verse. If Rothenberg stays close to the original, he nevertheless presents a modern reading, where Wittgenstein and existential views of language encounter the inexpressable "emptiness" of Zen in twenty-first century American idiom.

True Zen practice begins and ends with sitting, but does not neglect mental stimulation. Revisiting these 100 classic case studies, Rothenberg enlivens the process, and if he returns one to translations from the original, if his practice deepens another's practice, so much the better. Every mile is made of inches.

—*Sam Hamill*

CONTENTS

Endless wind, boundless moon—
     eyes arise within eyes.
Insatiable heaven, impossible earth—
     light remains beyond light.
Willows in darkness, flowers bright,
     Ten thousand homes on the road:
Knock at any door—
     someone will come to open it.

The Highest Truths

Bodhidharma secretly crosses the river.
You already know what's on the far side.

When you see smoke, you know there is fire.
When you see horns, you know there's an ox.

Hmm, this dimwit decides to speak up.
Bah! What he says is not worth a cent.
He won't lose the wild fox spirit!

Cross from west to east, and then east to west.
Let no one know which side you're on.

Inside one phrase you will see through to many.
It takes just one arrow to fell one eagle,
even one more will be more than you need.

Enough already, I'm clear to the other side. I ask:
What end is there to the pure wind, circling the earth?
Forget the target, up there in the heights of the truth.
That is one place where emptiness will never find you.

The End It Is Easy

To say the word "Buddha" is to muddy your boots.
Say the word "Zen," make your face full of shame.

When a fish swims by, the water is muddied
When a bird flies by, a few feathers fall.
This is normal enough:
Just don't love or hate, you'll be lucid with fear.

Who can then do it?
Do you ask me to live stone cold!?
An upside-down question:
How dare you speak of difficulty and ease!

Dragons murmur in trees long dead.
They may exist, they may be a dream.
In two choices there's no possibility,
in one there's no hope to choose—
consciousness and point of view, *chi* and *ching*.
See for yourself, know what you see.

So far I understand nothing.

When the Master Is Unwell

One tool, one thing, one sound, one space
it's all a way in or a scar on your face

This way will do, but that way will do too.
That way won't do, and this way won't do either.
Avoid each of these paths, and see
if there's anywhere else to go—
The climb of an unassailable steep blue cliff.

sun smiling shadow, moon smiling shadow
all two faces, always two faces

If you speak like this to sad people,
you will sadden them to death.

Carry Your Burden

In the real world, under bright light,
there's nothing to point out, nothing to lose
as long as the sickness fits the cure.

Carry your burden to the great hall
crossing from east to west and west to east.
Look around, there is nothing, no one is there—
do you want to be so completely revealed?

That visitor departed in rank disappointment,
she will leave the illusive wise city behind.
She will go to the top of a lonely peak
build a grass hut, live there, pass the time
deep with scorn for the rest of us.

A wild fox spirit? That's a wayward thing.
Even a cub knows the lion's roar.
Nothing can stop her from silencing
the tongues of all in the world.

So look down from there:
The scenery is lovely but the case is not complete.

A cat can subdue a leopard.
Or, reason can subdue a leopard.
Hard to tell what is meant, as the words are so close in Chinese.

The Grain of Rice

Grab this great earth with all of your fingers:
it's no bigger than one grain of rice.
Let the whole thing slip easily out of your grip
then strike the drum and you can't find the sound.

I can't let it go if I don't know how.
So smash the mirror before you will meet me.
Come see me only when your reflection is gone.

Enlightenment is nothing like a tree.
The mind or the mirror is not what it stands on—
polish, shine as much as you want,
you will find no roots.

If nothing is clear when all is swept clean,
then why wipe the dust away?

Every Day a Good Day

Every day a good day
From dawn to sunset
Days, months, years float by.

The frog jumps, but he can't leave the basket.

There is no single day when the good turned to bad.
There is no point in history when all went sour.
(You cannot blame our ills on the past.)

The rain has gone on, the clouds slink away
The road is like ice inside fire.
You make cascades silent,
and hear cicadas thrum
from deep within stone.

If you so much as move, thirty blows.
Take what's coming to you. Then get out.

Your Name as Answer

word before sound, worlds away
if you can't hear it you don't know it's there

Ask about Buddha,
the answer's just your own name

the pass to cross there
is not in the human world
outside the mind blue peaks fill our eyes

By the edge of what river will you find no wind?
the leaves are all blown by a different tune
How can there be such things?

In the wet country the wind no longer blows
In stillness the birds sing out from the thicket:
never the same song, never the same.
You ask the questions. You are who you are.

Eyebrows of the Wind

Learn only what you can use on the road
Don't get caught like a sheep behind fences
Choose words that follow the breeze in the grass,
shapes waiting like crouching lions.

When you meet someone else on the meandering road,
you can size up each other's illumination.

He who speaks asks if his eyebrows are still there.
You say: the eyes have it.
No blade of grass clings to your body.

Gates to All Directions

Gates to all directions,
leaving from and coming to the country.
A stranger comes, a neighbor goes
A traveler leaves and a brother comes home—
reflect the moment in a saber's blade

If it's not south, it's north.
If it's not west, it's east.
Nowhere is safe anymore.

There are thorns in the mud
There are frogs in the sea
There is something rather than nothing.

In the season of great peace you have no concerns.
Walk right through the gate, step out
from the forest of brambles;
clean, naked, bare, unscathed,
still a plain person, you will no longer cling
and imagine nothing is actually something.

Why so many gates? All open, open?
You can't smash them down with a hammer—
They are open!

All This Shouting

Look up—the sages suck in their breath
and swallow their voice
Look down—worms, maggots,
all the rest of us sentient beings
beam out a shining light.

Walk straight ahead—how will you deal?

After three or four shouts, a swipe at the head
Always let the monk make the first move
(all this violence, only, to cut away pride?)

Sometimes a shout is a crouching lion.
sometimes it is a jeweled sword.

Cut through the noise
Up! Down!
Slicing quick to the other side.

If there's no wound to enter,
you must find a way in,
Once through, you must not turn your back
to see where you are. Out!

It Takes a Word

One right word is all it takes
it can smash the chains and break down the gates
Who knows such words?
—Look around you and see,

What's the use of today?
shock the country, stir up the crowd
swallow all in one gulp and dwell in the clouds

Look back at that monk who could walk across water
Don't let him get away with it:
"You smug fellow, if I had known you could conjure up wonders,
I would have broken your legs!"
Then he who speaks disappears
 (he has said the word)

I hold up my palms with nothing to do
having heard the word, don't seek out the flock
they will only abuse it and get out of hand

cut through the clouds, walk inside rock, always say yes to work
the distant land is only seen when it peeks above the horizon
the glacier's waters cannot be held back—
they return to the waves of the sea

Three Pounds of Cotton

What is the Buddha?
"Three pounds of cotton."
—He points to a gingko to chastise a willow.

these three pounds are the road to the City
the West in the East
the forest that grows from a discarded staff
the robe of mourning, the secret code

a thousand years of unsold goods
nowhere to put them, no one to buy

If you cast your rod just to reel in dragons
you may pull in those who do know the self.

Flowering gardens, autumn forests,
color in time and the moods of the year.
The sun-raven rises, in his left eye, a half pound
The moon-rabbit runs, in his right eye, eight ounces
The same looks divergent in wandering light
When the answer strikes, the canyon welcomes the echo—
let the blind and the lame pass through.

Snow in A Silver Bowl

Clouds freeze in place over endless plains
but the world can still be seen.
Snow conceals the white petals,
still the flowers are there.

Cold as black ice, fine as rice powder
these reasons are moot:
pack the snow in a silver bowl

an outburst of occlusion

What do you say?
I'm here in a mouthful of frozen thought
seeing my breath in the air

Rout out the wind that ripples the flag;
The white heron walks in the bright night light.

The Appropriate Statement

A lifetime deserves an appropriate statement:
a sharp blade with no place for a handle
a rat chewing on raw ginger...

If you get it, you can go home and sit in peace.
Otherwise—accept the verdict:

breathing with life, the words are in our ears
standing apart like a mile high wall
it's lonely and steep, lonely and steep.

The appropriate phrase is the horn from the dragon
you wrenched off in the middle of night.
Tell me, where is the other horn?
How is it that you have just one?

There's no such animal, or if there is,
He jabs around in circles now.
When cornered on the straight and narrow road,
You have to know just what to say.

Upside-Down Phrase

the single sword kills and the double revives
the upside-down world is no longer here

jump all about, fall back three thousand miles
stretch out your body back in the wild reeds

do not use a question to ask a question
the answer is where the question is not
to get there you must ask another way

there are always three mysteries:
the mystery of the essence
the mystery of the phrase
the mystery of the mystery

The teacher can mirror insight in the clear
She must also be free to appear—and disappear

Adrift in the Weeds

Peace awaits through the forest of thorns.
There is one hand uplifting and one pressing down.

"I will break out, ask the Master to break in."
(If I weren't alive, they'd all laugh at me.)
He says: *"you too are adrift in the weeds."*

Walking the country, each step breaks in and out.
Traveling through time, marking manifold paths.
Leaving one place you will enter another.
Every place has a name, every house is a home.

The chick breaks out, the hen breaks in—
when the baby awakes, the egg is no more.
Mother and child both forgotten,
chirping in harmony on the same branch:
guide alone, serve alone.

First Come from the West

Do not flee from arrows or duck before swords
to explain when the spray floods the sky.

Why come from the West?
life in one place wears thin
(many people doubt this, it is so oft discussed)

If three people call the lampshade a turtle,
        then it's a turtle.
What hides underneath the tattered robe?
The flame of eternity scorches the hills.

You stare at a wall for nine fruitless years,
at last it is time, for the wind fans the fire.
Sitting too long, all will get tired.

Unload your baggage and walk far away,
spiraling back from it, kiss it goodbye.
The path it is lonely, and it takes many years
but it is there you must go.

Conjure the Temple

You can build the edifice just in your mind.
A single hand makes no random sound
A rough-hewn staff in the clear river—
no one sees you raise it out of the stream.

Above is the sky, below is the earth.
Have you heard about this?

Nothing can be seen of the stone but its shape.
The snake cannot coil in a currentless pool.
No illusions! Only truth in the eddies.

Where dragons swim, waves arise without wind.
You are safe in the stillwater;
layers on layers, shadows of shadows.
That's the way it looks to us,
that's the way it looks.

One Finger Zen

one speck of dust contains the world
bloom of the earth in a single flower

before it appears, how can you see it?
cut one blade of grass and all will die

If they ask you, give them the finger,
which finger to give is up to you;
with this silence you cut off all tongues here on earth—
snatch away everyone's voices on earth

warm and cold in heaven and hell
warm and cold inside you

cast a driftwood piece back into the ocean
once it drifted to you and then now you can't reach it

Swim in the surf and take in the blind turtles
Send them on to a world where no Buddhas are found
Empty it all, empty inside and out.

A blind turtle climbs through a hole in the driftwood,
Pulls himself up right out of the sea,

one finger pointing between you and he

Another One from the West

Your thoughts may pile up inside like mountains,
snowdrifts of silence ready to blow.
Someone may appear to start avalanches,
Shut his mouth so the word won't be said.

Whack your friends with cushions, no fear of a strike.
Trading with demons won't give you an edge.

Do today's monks still have blood under their skin?
The trip from the West may mean absolutely nil.
When has dead water ever hidden a flow?
No dragons, again, in the stagnant pool.
Watch for bubbles coming up, breath by the surface.

Counting the waves, sixty-two peaks of blue.
The afternoon clouds have not yet come together;
billowing mountains, all azure shades.
They block off your eyes, shut in your ears—
Back to the questions for thirty more years.

Lotus Flower, Lotus Leaves

to learn the sense of words beyond patterns

the weeds underwater are already blooming
the lotus on the surface is contained in the leaves

in the midst of words	*pass through words*
in the midst of meanings	pass though meanings

while gripping a tool pass through the tool
let yourself be at ease

foxdoubt, foxdoubt, no wonder without regret

(The wild foxes, uncertain, walk across the frozen river,
listening beneath for the sound of water.
If they hear nothing, they may cross to the other side.)

Turtle-Nosed Snake

Every one of us is a crossroads of danger.
There's nothing beyond the great beyond,
it's as fine as atomic dust.

Watch closely the turtle-nosed snake—
this is a spirit who sees a spirit, a thief who knows a thief.
Why gather then in a herd?
You must run with the pack to be one of them.

Fallen in the weeds! Where is the snake? I strike!
Raise your eyebrows to look and you won't see.
It's already gone by. Today I too have been bitten;
A tiger, a serpent, an arrow?
Don't look under his feet, but under your own.

Repeated words are not worth enduring.

On the Sacred Peak

With one word, one act, one meeting, one touch,
you will see whether someone is shallow or deep,
and know if they're facing forward or back.

They wander over endless mountains, and decide:
"Right here is the top of the sacred peak."
Oh? And look around—
Without the sun and rain these fields would be dead.

The earth goes on so long as it kills people with sadness.
Whoever you meet, you must take care.

"If I tell you what this peak is, you'll fall on flat ground!"
Must we all come down from our mountains?

When you get to the point of merging with nature,
the eye sees not itself
the ear hears not itself,
the hand feels not itself
the sword cuts not itself
the flame burns not itself,
so we need the other world.

Skulls will cover the ground, but who would know?
They won't live again. They will not look, listen, or touch.
The blade slices blazes, metal melts away.

roll around in the weeds at the top of the hill
how far from the top will you fall?

Lay Down and Rest

Well, the sea is calm, the river is clear
A dog brings the white flag of peace.

Two people held up by a single staff,
they call to each other, going and coming together.

days without worry, lazy blue mountains
in the heart of the water the jade rabbit jumps
down in the white clouds the gold dragon stirs

and we're high on the bluff beyond demons and villains
or deep in the sea where the Buddhas can't see us

arrive to the place, relax, and lie down.
There is time now for everything.

The Hermit Holds Up His Stick

Those who got here before me, why didn't they stay?
They had not gained enough strength on the road.
With my staff on my shoulder,
I leave others behind,
and go straight ahead to the myriad peaks.

Build an illusory city for falcons to roost
Ten thousand people are sitting right here
One or two will understand.
(If he looks at you from the back of his head, do not follow.)

Fading flowers, falling streams
look to the left—a thousand lives
look to the right—ten thousand years.

with the sound of footsteps come two more eyes
they watch from the silence and recognize ridges.
Why just right here?

Do not cling to cold ashes
don't hold onto strange plants on the cold cliff
and expect to pull yourself up.
I raise the stick and hold it high, here on the summit,
imagining millions, *face all like a dream.*

Alone on the Summit

And what's so special atop the mountain?
A swipe at the ear.
The time you take charge you will leap into life.

In the gate of expedience, sometimes roll out,
sometimes roll up, sometimes up in out, sometimes out in...
on the same path but not the same track.

better to turn from things than to chase them;
possible wheels can all turn both ways.
So—we descend.

Limbs Exposed to the Autumn Wind

See the rabbit and unleash the falcon
use wind to fan the flames—
What's it like to enter a tiger's lair?

What season is this? The family breaks up, the people scatter.
When leaves fall the body is exposed to the air.
Hold up the sky and carry the earth.
Clean, pure, even steps through the empty breeze.

You feel oncoming winds from the source of unrest.
These are the questions that use things.
An arrow flies far through the void.
Do you feel your hair standing on end?

The truth of things is always this obvious.
Is it subject or object? Quandary or awe?

Limbs left out in the autumn wind,
no leaves yet to cover them.
When you fuse all past and present
fools and sages, sky into earth,
and everything else, you will see
how these questions have helped us.

Unsaid Truths

Is there more to all this than what you have heard?
> *There is.*
And what is it that people have been denied?
> *Nothing, really.*
What?
> *I've already said too much.*

You've fallen too low this time,
frantic, hiding the body but showing your shadow.
> *That's the way it is.*

Say neither yes nor no to mind.
Say nothing.
Speak for no one.
Each guards her own land.
Hold onto your standards.
Keep those words out of sight.

Hang up your bowl
Call it quits for the day.
The wall-mirrors offer too many images.
Smash them, then I'll meet you.

The body is the tree of truth
The mind a smooth reflecting pool.
Do not blur it with dust and grease.
Keep it clean, wipe in circles from the center on out.

Enlightenment is not a tree
The mind is no more than broken glass.
There has never been more than this,
so let the dust settle in peace.

Just Go Along with It

Flames will destroy everything
at the end of the universe.
It may already be destroyed.

A cold cricket cries in the pile of wet leaves.
He wanders back and forth, unable to get past regret.

Go along with it
Stumble in rain,
Walk on alone.
At the end of the trail is a warm cabin with a single fire.
There you may dry out those lonely years.

Big Turnips

He's got his own road up through the skies.
His turnips are the biggest in the country!
But what has that got to do with anything?
Is the wheat beneath the mountain ripe yet or not?

If you so much as open your mouth, he'll snatch out your eyes.
If you know what's what, you'll chew your food, not gulp it down.
The swan is white, the crow is black,
that's not worth noticing, now, is it?

They did well to steal the eyes of travelers
Nothing's left of the body so no one can see.

The Body Returns

Move, a shadow appears.
Wake up, ice forms.
You, dragon, find water.
Tiger, talk to the mountain.

Circle the seat, shaking your head.
What is shook by the wind breaks down into dust.

This body of mine is made of four parts:
the skin and bones all return to the earth
the tears and blood all return to water
breath goes back to fire,
movement goes back to wind,
Where could this illusion I call myself be?

The Elder Stands Still

Stand still until the time is right—
so many people are lost when they move.

There's a man standing by who sees through it all.
He has completely attained another one's power.
He uses effort to make up for lack of skill.
He is always passing in and out through your senses.
His face turns yellow and green.
What can be done about the fact that there is such a man?
Strike once with a whisk, split the blossoming mountain to bits.
The whole world appears right now.
Its layers have fallen apart.

His doubt itself is a mountainous heap,
the pieces of his life discarded.
When he steps, the snowpack has started to melt,
when the sun is above no shadows are cast.

At night the fragile ocean sparkles with clumps of light:
Worry for the tangible world.

At Once Draw a Circle

Sometimes his eyes are like comets,
so would you agree he's awake?
Sometimes he calls south north,
but tell me, is he mindful or mindless?

My visit has already missed the point,
so he drew me a circle instead:
Do you see the immovable cage?
"Round and round the diamond turns, tinkling like jade.
Horses carry it up the plank, onto the waiting ship."

I'm used to fishing for whales in the great ocean,
what am I to make of a salamander in the wet sand?
Tell the turtle not to carry the mountains away,
for where can I look then to see waterfalls?

Come Down from the Mountains

Where have you just come from?
> *The mountains.*
By the tone of your voice, I am sure
You never found the right peak at all.

Though everyone in the world is the same,
it is still appropriate to ask;
If you want to know the mountain road,
you must be the one who travels it.

You learn the truth of someone by testing their speech.
Not even a fly will get past your scrutiny.
Why try so hard to be clever?

No single hair common,
no single strand sacred.
The whole earth has never concealed it.
No particular ever reveals it.

when cold, no sense of cold.
when old, no sense of old.

What Happened Back There?

Is it black? Is it white?
Is it crooked? Is it straight?
How will you know?

Where I come from people take no notice of rules.
This is still news: A truthful man is hard to find.
Give me back the words. (And we can't let him go.)

One phrase never settled this man's query.
To this day he's still one who sleeps in the fields.

Please watch under your feet!
The tea bowl falls into a thousand pieces.
Who said you could speak to the mountains like that!?

Wandering Senses

I smelled the new grasses and followed the flowers.
How else to know spring!
Yes, it was more than autumn dew.
Have you ever written any of this down?
Not yet.
When you have time, you should try to.

The earth is cleared of all dust and haze—
Whose eyes do not open?
A lone crane lands on a naked tree,
a monkey screams on the crumbling terrace.
A man in the woods can still draw the bow
after the thief has run away.

My shirt is in tatters, my pants have no zipper.
I started all this to help others,
who would think I'd end up a blathering idiot?

After this: *whose* eyes would not open?

This Triple World

Don't wait around when lightning strikes
When thunder comes there's no time to hide

there are ghosts before you, they won't go away

Once the arrow leaves the bow, it will not come back.
The moonshadow strikes the archer at night.

There is nothing in this triple world
Nothing one, two, three times or more.

The white clouds are a ceiling.
the stream plays the world like a lute,
one pluck, three strings, no one sings along.
All the tones may be clear,
but when you hear them, you're mute.

When the rain has passed, the river is deep.
Dragging in mud, dripping in water,
run from the thunder, no time to sleep.

Eighty four thousand verses,
eighty four thousand to go.

The Iron Ox

a gradual sweep against the grain
seven ways down and eight across
To a quick person, a word
To a quick horse, the blow of a whip.
At such a moment, who is the master?

He seems to be right, but he's not really right.
You know that the eyes of the bystander see.

If you don't chase the lost sheep,
crazy comments cease.
Instead you come here with verses!

On the road show your sword to a swordsman
Offer poetry only to poets
Stand away from your poems and try out that sword a little:

The Iron Ox straddles the river,
built to hold back the flood.
The great waves rise up a thousand feet
billowing whitecaps fill up the sky—
and only a single shout is needed
to make them turn and head for the source.

Flowering Vines

At work on the road you're a mountain tiger.
In the laws of the world you're a caged monkey.
If you want more then get out, come down.

Sometimes he stood still like a ten mile high wall.
Sometimes he cut a path for you,
died with you and lived with you.

If you learn the live words, you will never forget.
If you learn the dead words, you won't save yourself.

the truth's like the moon in the water
there's no way through the whirlpool
twisted thoughts—still words in our ears

Size up the audience before you begin.
Pluck on the harpstring, pick out the tune.
The string is not fretted, the place is not marked.
You have to know just where to strike
and catch the petals as they fall.

It's Like a Dream

Stop right in your tracks, and the steel forest blossoms.
Is there room for this?

"Heaven, Earth, and I are but one.
One seed between me and the myriad things!"
See that flower?
People these days say it's a dream

The ultimate person is formless and hollow
yet all the myriad things are his fault!
They are us, we are they, and no one can tell.
Each different but made some way one and the same.

When it's hot, all is hot, when it's cold, shivers all around.
(Except when night is light, when wrong is right.)
Merge difference with sameness and judgment is tough.

Lead me to the edge of a thousand foot cliff,
give me that extra push to the void.
Or: if you were pushed down on level ground,
life itself could still not be ceased.

It's not so easy to end it, to blend all into mush.
There's never just one thing, always more,
(an axe handle with no place for the blade)

The frosty moon sets, the night's nearly over.
In the weeds at dawn, a fine mist cover.
The world has returned it, and left all to see.

Is there anyone else there?
(If they did not sleep in the same bed,
how could they both know the cover is worn?)

Do not use a mirror to see mountains and rivers.
If you do you will need to divide them in two.
Leaning over to look at the deep, clear pool—
do you bounce back in tandem or all by yourself?

To Die a Great Death

Even the wise can't always tell
where right and wrong are mixed.

A man stands out from the crowd:
He scratches thin ice like a unicorn's horn
He burns like a lotus on fire.

After the great death, how will he come back to life?
Only by daylight, never the dark

There are such things! A thief knows to strike the rich.
Seeing a cage, he makes a cage.
A flute with no holes strikes the soundboard of silence.

How is it before the rooster has crowed?
The sound does not exist.
And how is it after the crow's time has gone?
Each knows the time for himself.

If you want intimacy, ask no questions.
The eye blinks in death the same as in life.
Even the ancients have never arrived.
I don't know who scatters dust in the sand.
If it's you, *now is the time to stop.*

Perfect Snowflakes

An inaudible wind circles the entire earth.
The snowflakes fall nowhere but here.

Who does not call the many things his companions?

You roll in the snow, you roll the snow in a ball.
You throw the snowball and wait for it to be caught.

The snowball hits its mark!
Clean eyes, clean ears
Chop wood, carry water

the snow is falling, faintly through the universe
            it belongs right here
and it makes the place look, in the end, like any other.

Not Cold, Not Warm

All obstructions removed, the whole appears everywhere.
The edges of temperature easily kill.
Too hot, too cold, fragile beings will die.

If not this season, then maybe the next.
Grifters sell sham silver cities.

In the heart of the first night, before the moon's out
they can't see each other—
both closed in a freeze over previous days.

From nothingness there's one road rambling from dust
past the eloquent silence of long ago.

No fire, no ice.
No smoke out of drowned coals.
I'll hide in the cauldron, I'll live in the cooler.
I'll fight my demons with more of the same.

How to Beat the Drum

How to go beyond study and teaching?
Learn how to beat the drum.
What's the real truth?
How to beat the drum.
To receive a man back from the beyond?
Beat the drum.

A metal spike. Barbed-wire fence. Iron filings. *Hard, hard.*
Pieces of steel, wrecked cars, rusting engines. *Hard, hard.*

In the morning to India, evening to China,
high and low over mountain paths.
you've been wandering footloose far too long,
You won't see through to get lost in the clear...

Beat the drum, beat the drum hard.

The Seven Pound Shirt

The many return someday to one.
And what will the one become?

I once made a seven pound shirt.
It was also a silver mountain.
Or an iron wall.

Don't use objects to teach us.

I wrap everything up in the ancient garment
and toss it into the western lake.
Who will share my shivering bare in the wind?

Wrapped up, all my hopes are drowning together—
You can only rest after you've won.

Rain Falling Sound

On thin ice, running over nails—
from inside the form of sound,
he walks above the sound of form.

Outside the gate the raindrops sing.
The inversion of beings, losing themselves, following after things.
What about you?
I almost *lose myself.*
What does that mean?
Speaking is easy, expressing the whole has *to be hard.*

What else can you call the sound of rain?
the chafing of atoms
the drench of the sky
the return of the oceans
the drizzle electric.

It may be a quail hanging upside down.
(The hall is empty but everyone's here.)
There's killing and caring, catch and release,
If ever you say he's let the streams enter.

Clouds brew back of mountains, storing the downpour.
Mark moon with finger, but finger's no moon;
Your feet tread the ground before you can reach here.

Six Is Not Enough

Does the sky need to speak for the seasons to turn?
Does the earth need to shout for things to be born?
Essence above, action below.

Six is not enough—*This is indeed a hard one.*
Is it the six senses? Is it the interrupted count?
One, two, three, four, five…
(Go all the way though, and then start again)
Every water drop now a crystal of ice;
There is no stair from the one to the many.

Flip the Teapot

Under the kettle the spirit of tea;
It's cool when warm, warm when cool.
You won't find it brewing the deadness of words,
but you may have luck in your life when you speak.

So drink the tea, say these phrases aloud:

A rope descends in a well on a moonlit night.
This kind of peachpit sprouts once in a thousand years.

Do you wash the rice to remove the sand,
or wash the sand to remove the rice?
Sand and rice are removed together.
What will the great congregation eat?

All the people of the world take a beating together.
The monks of the world have no place to go.
Thunder shouts down from an empty sky,
however you crash through the field.

Eluding the Net

What do fish eat after passing the net?
When you come through the net then I'll tell you.

The goldfish, escaped, is finally free.
He leaps in the air and startles the crowd.

One exit, one entry,
one thrust, one parry
one capture and one release—
there is neither victory nor defeat.

Once past the water, he jumps over clouds:
One thunderclap brings the purest wind.
He's up where the thousand-foot waves spray the sky;
Still, he has nothing for dinner.

Concentration

What is concentration:
Food in bowl, drink in glass

A bag of sharp nails.
Gold sifted in sand.
From inside the palace, no one sees past the walls.
He draws in his tongue,
Those who know the law fear it.

Each grain of rice is round,
each drop of water is wet.

The sun's over the ridge, yet still the day's dark.
The mist melts away but the valley is dim
And the travelers all have no clothes.

The Last Word

The last word

> It came before all others.
>
> If you look at it now you'll go blind.

is meant for you;

> Tongue to the ground.
>
> Head with no tail, tail with no head.

light and dark, dark and light, pair by pair, utterly two—

> No path between this one and that.
>
> You're headed southeast, I will go northwest.

In the depths of the night, both trapped at the ice, on the thousand crags.

> Ten days to go,
>
> covered with snow,
>
> filling the channels and gullies:

The last word is meant for you.

Walk the Plank

I expected a stone bridge,
but there's only one log felled over the stream.

The solo path brings danger,
the log extends through the clouds.
Roll the tree over and no one can cross—
neither profane nor sacred will come.

People of power don't come by twos and threes.

Mountains smashed into bits become dust
on the floor of the oceans—
All we can do is pound waves on the foot of the cliffs
And swim the white surf through which no one can see.

Wild Ducks

Wild ducks, coming together,
who knows where they go?

They told me of the clouds on the mountain
and the moon all over the sea.

They've flown away.
You wanted to fly away too.

Don't make me speak,
There's nothing to say.
Don't let a wild duck cry.

Hold Out Two Hands

Deftly passing through birth and death,
he may now set tools in motion.

Slice through iron, pierce through steel.
Wrap around heaven, wrap around earth.
A tentative pole, a fan of reeds—
Hold out the silent hands.

All of us on the planet lose out at once;
The wind whispers all through the world.

Condolence Call

If you're close to reality, you can turn things around.
Is there a way to draw an unbroken path?

You come to the door for a condolence call:
Tap the coffin and ask,
"Alive or dead? Tell me right now."
I won't say, I won't say.
"Then what are you doing?"
Looking for relics of the Master.
"Waves spread far, clouds flood the skies. What else do you want?"
Heavens! Heavens!

He buys the hat to fit your head.
He pours water down on you.
He comes close to take you.
In the heavens and on earth,
he's found life in death—
smooth sailing from here on.

Does everyone see them? They flash like lightning.
Whose worn out sandals are these?

Rabbits and horses with horns! How bizarre! *Chop them off.*
Oxen and rams without horns! How bizarre! *Chop them off.*
You may fool others, but what pattern is that?

White foam fills the skies, where can relics be hid?
They won't fit in your eyes or your ears.

Hardly a memory, barely a wisp—
Clouds like mountains, turn like peaks.

Through Three Targets

The Buddhas have never been in this world.
There is nothing for the people to know.
They search outside themselves and miss the cavern
        of tangled vines.

How does the arrow pass through three targets?
There's capture. Release. Wind bending grass.
Swirl against current, why wait any longer?

The winning shot strikes
nowhere near the three targets.
Inside the arrow is the focused aim,
the dream of exactness where defect creeps in.

Strike an eye, and the ears go deaf.
Lose an ear, and the eyes go blind.
The course of the dart is clear.

Don't Pick or Choose

The right path is easy,
Just don't pick or choose.

Mountains will crumble, rocks will fall
Deep as the ocean, firm as the earth.
A mosquito flies in the fiercest of winds.
An ant tries to uproot an iron pillar,
picking, choosing, no, do not decide—

A cloth drum hiding,
making no sound.
The boom disappears in the empty space.

Cannot Explain

Don't pick or choose—what a cliché!
You won't get it for thirty more years.
Walk the balance beam, solid as steel.
Do not judge others against yourself.

An ape eats a wax worm, a mosquito pierces the iron ox.
Animal, animal. A dragon slips into water, a tiger heads
    for the hills.
The raven flies, the rabbit runs, from night until day.
From past and from present, buried alive—all at once.
Where will we end up without choice?

Thick as Pea Soup

Water poured on you keeps you dry.
Wind gusting stops at your door.
It's like empty space—solid, impervious.
Address your plea to the sky!

"Cover your ears," he draws back;
stops the words in their tracks.
"Stand on one foot," thus respond in silence.

See yourself in him,
see his idea in you.
Skim over the grasses, slide over the spears.
No blood, no breeze.

Why the Two Sides?

Buddhas and the rest of us, we are the same.
Mountains and rivers and inside the self...
Why then divide it all up?

Get the words turning, natural bridge,
not enough to let go of the need to hold on.

But if you don't let go, no part of the earth
is at all worth grasping, grasping at all.

Change my staff to a dragon and swallow the world.
In all ten directions there are no walls.
On all four sides there are no gates.
How will you handle this one?

Do not speak of peach flowers floating on water.
There's no grasping clouds, or seizing the fog.
You may say it again ten thousand times,
but that's nothing like catching it once in your hands.

"If you have a staff, I'll give you a staff.
If you have no staff, I'll take yours away."

Politics

Just tell me how you'll take the heartland all by yourself.
I'll set it up on a speck of dust.

Light shines everywhere—what good is the nation?
I stand like a mile-high wall,
There is no house divided.
Give me my words back, I'll admit you are free.

Tough to placate the folk if you want them to think.
The old ones keep their furrowed brows,
Wise rulers are not to be found.
The people are few, and you hardly meet them.
But do not point to yourself:
The perfect world has never been.

A Jewel Within

Inside heaven and earth
past space and time
there is a jewel
in the mountain's form.

everyone is perfectly whole

Come out of your cave,
before you miss it.

Look! Above!
Clouds move on.
Hundreds of shapes, piled on high.
(Cut them off.)
Lapping of water, boundless sea
Left, right, blocking the mind
White moon-drenched flowers, see for yourself
Go blind when you see them,
Meeting the end of words.

The Famous Dead Cat

Holding up the mewling beast:
Speak, or it will die!

When you can't explain, then you must cry.
Where you can't speak, there you must look.

The right word would have saved the cat.
That time no one really died.
At an impasse—revolution;
changed, you pass through.

No one spoke up, they were either
too quick, or not quick enough.

The creature held up,
reason sliced in two.

The kitten run over on the line in the road.
A casualty, an answer, a tear.

The Cat Could Have Lived

I took off my sandals, placed them on my head.
If you had been there, you could have saved the cat.

Of like hearts, like minds,
You two on the same road would know that.

You may murder the cat, it's none of my business.
The sandals don't purr, and torn they won't scream.

If someone dies for them these puzzles matter.
You must try to care, if you wish to live.

Ask from Outside

The monk wonders not of the said and the silent.
Like a horse, he turns at the shadow of whips.

Where I strike with the staff there's a glistening eye.
If you think it is gold, pass it through fire.
If you have a mouth, learn how to consume it.

Stop for a second, you slip back to square one.
Ten thousand miles away, just then
the stranger knows neither here nor there, yes nor no.

Three secrets from the summit: *drink tea, take care, rest;*
Forests of pattern cleanly revealed.
The single eye untangles past from future.
He chased a dog to the fence, what to do but return?
Retreat, retreat,
back from the thousand league chase after wind.
The horse runs over and rustles no dust up,
At once he is there,
Snap your fingers three times,
At once you can call him back.

Your Just Desserts

Adjusting to light, adapting to darkness,
a pit for a tiger, surprise for a thief.

He knows where he comes from, but he will not tell.
If you travel like this, then death will catch you,
and demand that you pay up your bills.

For thirty years I have handled horses,
but today I've been kicked by a mule!

He did not say where he comes from,
he'll need to wake up on his own.

Shake the Seat

Shake the desk, shake the seat—
That's all I will say.

Do not sleep in the birch grove,
find the desert and make dust out of dust.

If you want marvels, look at the gray skies:
No Buddha above, no sentience below.
Appear in the world, know mist clarifies;
lucidity in the darkest clouds.

What Is Your Name?

My name is your name.
Each macaque wears an ancient mirror:
It was never described until now.

To ride tigers you must be completely sure—
Stir the wind of lament, laugh the poison laugh.

His laughter ends, I know not where he's gone.
I do not even know what to call him.

Sitting Inside the Circle

There is no place to bite it.
He sat down in the circle and would not go on.

What's going on in his mind?
Call it awareness, and it's already changed.

One grips, one releases
one ends, one begins,
one life, one death.

Shoot the monkey, circle the tree.
Who has ever hit a moving target?

Stop climbing and the peak won't be found.
Reach the top and see only more mountains.
The road does not end—the earth is round.
Inside the world one sits still.

Dustless, trackless, naked and clean.
Such a path cannot help but beckon:
but each of you, please, watch your own steps.

Refusing to Speak

One crack of the whip
One thought—
ten thousand years

How will you speak with your mind and mouth shut?
Eons of silence; I have lost my descendants.

On all continents Spring soon will end.
The sun shines through the sea on the forest of coral.
Razor-sharp blossoms, color down deep.
The blue below surface,
through calm beneath waves.

Still Staying Silent

With your mouth sealed, what will you say?
You should cease from asking and also be silent.
When there's no one here, I'll cover my eyes,
and stare straight to you.

Past the boundless horizon a kingfisher soars
He admits to the target:
I hit when he's flown past.

Miraculous arrows.
One strike fells an eagle.
No chance of escape.
No sense of the bullseye, no sharp-pointed question.
No praise, no blame, no speech, no answer.

My whole body is stuck in the mud.

Cold Cloud Swim

Stick to the skin, cling to the bones,
Wake up with a silent voice kept in.

I have lost the screen of the future,
through which the past is seen.

Inside mute subtlety only clouds.
Mix dirt in the river,
shock the body awake
with a cool plunge in the deep.

Assent and Deny

For the truth, you need not explain or teach
There is nothing to hear and no destination.

Nearly all of us suffer from this kind of malaise
At the mercy of someone else;
Obscurity extends forever.

They say that white stands for merging in brightness,
black for merging in darkness
Most people instead are absorbed in schemes.

In the vast country there is but one road.
You will run your footsteps down it.
In the future you will come up with a phrase
that will blanket everyone here on Earth.

Want Some Rice?

How can one stay where the spirits linger?
All seekers, come eat!
But take care—
butter turns quickly to poison.
Rice holds fast like a white cloud.
Think twice before you ask for this kind of food.

No Reason to Hit

It's not easy, in words,
to tell shallow from deep,
and know who is guilty
and who needs to suffer.
Be more than example,
logic is no joke.

There is one way in and one way out,
as host or guest, you welcome the challenge.
To gather is easy,
To disperse is hard.
Wood calls for termites,
mirages encircle the sea.

It has been our purpose
to pull out pegs, and loosen nails,
to set thoughts free and untie what is bound.
This lets people loose where there's nothing to hold.
The ancient shore crumbles,
the ocean dries up.
The mind is last to go.

What's for Lunch?

It's impossible to have come from nowhere.
Have you eaten yet?
Yes I have.
Would you say that I'm blind?
The same as your eyes.

I dreamed a white light filled the room.
This is an omen of getting to zero.
Each wanted to test the other:
The divine and the human wash ashore as one.

Piece of Cake

The hawk nabs the pigeon.
Turtles hide in their shells.
There's thunder on earth.
The tongue curls to the roof of the mouth.

You ask about leaving the triple world,
you reach for the three sides to see.
Too many ask about transcendent talk,
and the Earth kills with sadness once more.

The Basis of Water

One day they awoke to the basis of water.
Suddenly soaked, crashing down walls.
The absence of anything that does not flow
subtlely leads to illumination.

It's just like remembering a dream in a dream!
A slap in the face, so sleepers awake,
like layers of sediment splashed upon mud;
the lines in the rocks, the hues in the canyon below.

All Sounds are Sounds

Is it true that all sounds are the voice of the Buddha?
Sure, it is true.
So would the master please stop sounding like a pile of shit?

A sure path to a beating, this line of inquiry.
How pathetic, these people at play in the sea!
In the end they'll collapse and drift out with the tide.

The sound of death, defecation, release to the earth.
It's useless to stop and think.
Shake the seat of your pants,
find a place to sit down and establish your lives.

A Newborn Baby

Is a newborn baby able to see?
Like throwing a ball onto swift-running water
Even a kingfisher cannot impale it.
Whose baby is he talking about?

Mountains still mountains, rivers always rivers.
He blurs all senses to one.
He uses no tools.
He covers everything deft as the sky.
He moves like the sun and the moon, never stopping.
In the midst of a stagnant haze, he is able to act.

Moment to moment, unstoppable flow.
If I call baby the path, you would misconstrue;
Consistently babbling from beginning to end.
Drifting away, you'll grow up blind.

Shoot the Elk of Elks

How to decide which elk to kill?
Look—an arrow! He let himself fall.
Though he lived for three steps, after five he must die.

One hand lifts the spirit, the other presses the body down.
If he ran a hundred miles his life still would be over.

The leader of the pack will be the last to go.
He guards his herd without losing poise.

And where's the arrow that gives life?
You aim for the ground instead of the beast.
The elk of elks raises his horns.
One arrow fells the hunter, who cannot run.
His own herd would be invincible.
But he needs only three steps to survive.

Fix your gaze high:
There might be a wingèd tiger, a panther with horns,
or an impervious moose who will keep out of range.

The hunter and the hunted both know how to look.
                    Their gaze shifts:
Over there, the twang of a bow!

Hard Fast Real

You need a good eye to thread fishing line.
Only experts know tools outside plans.
Bodies all waste away, the hard and fast lie elsewhere.
On the mountain, flowers gleam like jewels;
the streams run indigo blue.

I suppose it is all right to break things up,
(That flute without holes strikes the felt sounding board.)
Yet the whole cannot be broken.
It's like catching the moon in a butterfly net:
To ask is to answer, to catch is to throw.

Standing under the fiercest winds,
Even the juniper berries freeze down.
The flute still sounds true as winds blow 'cross its edge—
The registers crack, the harmonics break.
The song needs no words to reply.

Thunk, thunk, the sound sways from the line
banging against the soft tree.
And the breeze blows over at last in the end,
rising whistles out over pure space.

The Ancients and the Pillar

The ancients merged thought with the column of stone.
A thousand years later, the plaster cracked open—
Not a drop falls.

People these days make a living from feelings.
As soon as you look for them,
you've bound your hands and feet.

In Korea they've already gone into the hall.
In China they haven't yet beaten the drum.
Give me back the story. Who wants to know?

Who says gold is like garbage?
The road is hard, there is joy in pain.
Pain in joy, wide open spaces, paths to the clouds.

Completely Exposed

There is nothing that "is" can affirm.
There is nothing that "not" can negate.
Free the yes from the no, strip yourself bare.

Cast all away, be completely exposed.
This state is what you must learn to trust.

What's he say?
he can fool you
What's he say?

He's withered and dying, but he returns
to a single room that is always swept clean.
It stands in a house
by duality's gate.
It guards the gap between something and nothing.

Search long without finding,
Nowhere else to look.
Even if the whole world—mountains, rivers, oceans, lakes,
grasses, flowers, roots, and trees—were turned into
a single gold lion,
you still wouldn't see it in front of your nose.

Roaring Tiger

This guy's an expert in playing with shadows.
He piles error on error. He's got teeth and claws.
His laugh cuts like a sword.
He lets go while still holding on.

If you don't strike when you see him,
You'll regret the moment for ten thousand miles.
Stripes on fur, but no claws or teeth?
I'll talk to you when your roar is ready.

The vast howl will shake up the earth.
Take the tiger's tail and pull on his whiskers.
Born together, die together,
Slap him across the ear.

Your Own Light

The surge is held back with the lightest touch,
He obstructs all the rivers, keeps no drop for himself.
Everyone has a light, but if you try to see it,
It's faint and far away.

Nothing's as good as nothing.
When people these days hear the word "light"
They ask at once:
Where is the food?
Where's the way out?

In the daylight we come and go,
anywhere as anywhere.
Suddenly it's midnight and there's no sun or moon—
In a place you've never been,
it's impossible to go on.

But in darkness there's light,
though it's not for us to see.

When the leaves fall, the tree has no shadow.
It's just a sketch drawn on the sky.
The absence of things is the same as things.

Sickness Cancels Out Cure

Sometimes a summit is covered in moss.
Sometimes the top is all rock and snow.
The climber does not need to live there—
he only wants to touch it:
But the peak is not worth more than any other place.

If the whole world is your tonic,
then what is it that ails you?

The radish is tart to the core.
The melon is sweet to the seeds.

Is there a way to climb down?
Sickness and health cure each other.
In one night we have melted the glaciers to drink.

Blind, Deaf, Mute

Blind, deaf, mute—no one can come near.
Soundless, without any play to the form
Can you make a choice?
What has that got to do with it!
laughing, crying
in dark and in light
Blind one! A true artist leaves no trace.
Deaf one! Let go of the point of words.
Mute one! Stick with the home of silence.

He could hear the ants fighting behind the mountain.
One chord on his lute and he knew we would lose.
The fall of the leaves, the bloom of the flowers,
Each marks the time under empty windows.

Tossing and Turning

If you were just an eye, you still couldn't see it.
If you were just an ear, you still couldn't hear it.
If you were just a mouth, you could not speak it.
If you were just a mind, you would not perceive it.

Now with no eyes, how would you see?
With no ears, how would you hear?
With no mouth, how could you speak?
With no mind, how can you think?

Clutching a pillow in the middle of night
All over the body are hands and eyes
all through the body are hands and eyes

Before Sound

No one has told us the one phrase before sound.
The single thread is still unbroken.

What is the body of wisdom?
　　　　　　An oyster gobbles the moon.
What is the purpose of wisdom?
　　　　　　A rabbit gets pregnant.

Without a moon, the pearls are few.
The moon comes out, rabbits swallow the light.

This mindmoon alone and full—

People these days just stare,
drive spikes into empty space.
One sliver of empty air,
ties your self to the place.

'

Rhinoceros Encircled

Bring me that fan of rhinoceros horn!
It's broken.
Well, then, get me the rhinoceros.
It's horn will be broken.
I like a beast who's missing his horn.

I drew a circle surrounding the word:

Ah, why did you not bring this out before?
It's under his nose.
Hold back, it might be dangerous.

The purpose is worth nothing without the source.
The rhino horn fan has long been in use:
cool in summer, warm in winter.
All of us have one, so why don't we know?

The boundless breeze and the horn on the head.
Just like we can't chase clouds after rain
or catch smoke once it has risen away.
The idea's in the circle, it could be controlled.
But you cannot cool flights of the soul.

Please Take Your Seats

It's hard to find someone who can guess the tune
the moment the first note is heard.
Let the hawk go when he sees a hare,
the suddenly swiftest is caught.

As for summing all words in a single phrase,
grabbing the universe in just one point,
dead and alive at once the same time—
      who can take it?

Climb down from your throne,
Give the next guy a chance.

Wild Fox Spirit

Do not deceive us, you wild fox spirit.
Try not to stray from the path.
Who says yellow leaves are not golden?
Who says a grazing shot cannot hit the bullseye?
He draws a cat according to plan.
He suggests only a single road.
We meet one alive while neglecting his phrases.
The wild fox stays curious just to survive.
The wild fox spirit is not ready for practice,
even after all this time.

Just as bright leaves charm children like trinkets,
the teachings claim an end to the people's confusion,
though ultimately none of them are true.

Invisible Sight

None of you left sees the words before sound.
When I can't see, why don't you see my not seeing?
It's not a thing, and it's nothing but you.

My sight, invisible,
guarded like a vanishing wall.
When you reach it, you cannot explain,
or even find the way on a map:
total indulgence at the start of the journey,
total restraint in the end.

Like an antelope grabbed by the horns,
feel the edge of the wall—
Its end could be anywhere, at any time.
Every atom in every place,
lies already halfway there.

Go Drink Tea

Run from the Buddha,
Run from the absence of Buddha.
Weeds will ensnare you if you don't flee.

A sleeping dragon does not see the still water.
Around him the breakers arise without wind.
When he goes then the moon comes, waves lap away.
Hide from the crowds, sail the ocean alone.
The sea swells up, ripples angle the clouds:
only in such tempests are dragons concealed.

How can you question a deaf man who hears?
Go   drink   tea.
Raise one cup to the sky.

Gold, Wood, Mud

A gold Buddha cannot pass through the forge
A wood Buddha cannot pass through the fire
A mud Buddha cannot pass through the water

Weeds ten feet deep in front of the chamber
If you pass through these verses you will need to know all

The mud one dissolving, returning to water,
seeing a rabbit, releases a hawk.
One misconstrues, fooling ten thousand people,
adding error to error—you glimpse its name.
Who would not try to carve a replacement?

Clouds are steamed rice
Pancakes on the flagpole
Monkeys pitch pennies at night

The gleaming one will only melt,
singeing his eyebrows.
You can't sink your teeth in him;
Melting, glowing, cooling away.
Above the head, below the feet—
boundless, boundless.

Catch the thief! Catch the thief!
Caught him! Caught him!
(Master, it isn't me.)

Charring embers, he did not make it.
Burned up! Only you can know.
Smoke and charcoal, what then is left?
There's one who's turned away from his self.

The furnace explodes.
The fire dies out.
The water dries up.
We pass.

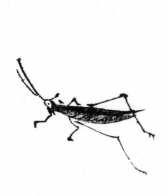

The Scorn of the Time

When heaven changes to earth,
the sky tumbles down, lakes go belly-up.
Cliffs fall over like a teapot cracking
beneath the weight of the tea.

Our own scorn smothers the history of evil.
The latest snow obscures the last.
Boiling water still melts ice.

I always turn the answers around in my fingers.
I urge you to stop before reaching the end:
You must check if the words are still emitting light.

A jewel in the palm reflects rays to the sun.
You lose it at once when it's cast in the waters,
not for friend nor for enemy,
know me or fool me,
all lies open to you.

Travel on Foot

Assembling causes, making results
Completing beginnings, unpacking ends.
Face to face, I cannot fool you:
Basically I have never explained.
"All summer we've asked, but you've told us nothing."
"When you wake up, then I'll tell you."

This guy's like a tortoise dragging its tail.
Already he's fallen halfway behind.
He does not know where to rest.
He gropes without grasping.
He adds frost to snow.
He constantly checks the map.
He said it was wrong to walk all this way.
Wearing out sandals, what is the use?

One brush stroke blots it out.
One leap takes you there.

The Play of the World

Mist comes up when the dragon howls.
Wind blows in with the roar of the tiger.
Gold and jade tumble together.
All arrowheads strike the common goal.

The play of the world runs from past through to future.
It fills all containers and spills them all out.
Those are its qualities, so what is it?

Within formless light you'll always be free.
Do not toy with your spirits, or they won't be revealed.
By night three thousand worlds are all still and silent.
Step out of the matrix and into the field.

Take my hand and come circle the One Certain Mountain.
We'll sadden ourselves not to death, but to life.

One Final Thing

All this time entangled
in the simplest things,
I know I am hopeless.

There still is the phrase around heaven and earth
and the phrase that cuts off streams.
There still are the words that follow the waves
While there is *nothing* in this triple world.

test the blade of a sword on a strand of hair
if the hair snaps
                    the sword is sharp
if the sword breaks
                        that's some strand of hair

Packing, hauling, bushels away.
I've brought up one hundred blue stories:
What sand have I thrown in your eyes?

Blue Cliff Record is a translation of *Pi Yen Lu* in Chinese. It is one of several classical collections of koans that make up the canon of study in the Ch'an Buddhist tradition, the Chinese ancestor of what would become Zen in Japan. The name refers to the place where it was written, but the Blue Cliff could just as well be anywhere, the mass of heaven and earth, the material of which the world is formed, all around us, and inside us.

The original text is not written as a poem, but as a series of cases, introduced and followed by detailed, baffling commentaries of various Chinese Buddhist masters compiled in the tenth and eleventh centuries. It is a dense and confusing document, with layers of recurring images, obscure footnotes, inclusions of ancient verse and references to distant miracles, all for the point of disengaging the student from mundane reality, unhinging us to be ready to be trained for the difficult ascent toward the truth.

The original *Blue Cliff Record* is a training manual for the most rigorous and predetermined kind of Zen study. So what right have I to meddle with it? None whatsoever. I have read and written purely as an outsider, as a seeker on my own path to pull apart logic and find something also as exact, but to my senses more beautiful, resonating with an ephemeral quality, barely traceable as part of the inscrutable truth. (Zen, as well, encourages a certain haughty defiance in the presence of the Masters. Risks are there to be taken.)

I have often sensed this resonance in the apocryphal koans of Zen, familiar with their haiku-like reductions in the versions of D.T. Suzuki and Paul Reps. One could say that it is worthless to those outside the rigorous course of study it constantly recommends. But the literature of religion extends far beyond its most stringent practices.

Whatever we believe, however we practice, the world offers thousands of documents of faith for our consideration. Zen logic suggests a pulling apart of the rules of language. Philosophy in our time has suggested the same. Wittgenstein has written that philosophy in the future should be composed poetically, and that future is now arriving. The kind of insight the *Blue Cliff Record* encourages is both free and exact at once.

My version is an attempt to get at the essence of each case, not repeating each koan and subsequent commentaries in the same form each time, but playing with the images in each story to pull out the form of concern.

Each tale is a dilemma, with no easy way out. It is a mood, it is the model of a situation we are to carry within us all the time, in case we may need it to work through a problem, or to see through a cloud.

The three existing scholarly translations have all been essential for framing my strange outsider's gloss on the material: *The Blue Cliff Record*, the original three volume work by Thomas Cleary and J.C. Cleary, (Shambhala, 1977, reprinted in one volume in 1992), Katsuki Sekida's *Two Zen Classics* (Weatherhill, 1977), and Thomas Cleary's slimmed-down new version, *Secrets of the Blue Cliff Record* (Shambhala, 2001).

I have been seeking the poetic possibilities of these tales now for several years. Revising the words, we lose our attachments to the words. I read them again—in my echoes they are always changing, ready to sound different once more.

—DR

The book is typeset in Goudy Old Style (Adobe version), by Frederick W. Goudy in 1915. The capitals are based on lettering found on a Renaissance painting. Goudy hoped when designing the lower case that it would be "in perfect harmony with classic capitals which harked back to a period some hundreds of years earlier." Eighty-five years later it remains a highly favored face among book designers.

The woodcuts in this book, in the designer's collection, come from the Juchikusai Shogafu (The Ten Bamboo Model Book), Chinese edition, 1879. Revised by Chang Hseuh Keng. 8 vols. The illustrations are intructional and intended to be used by artists as models. This is a very humble version of a centuries-long tradition of model books of astonishing visual merit and importance.

1500 copies printed by Thomson-Shore Inc.

Cover and book design consultant: Martin Moskof